Grandma

A HOUSE NEEDS A GRANDMA IN IT.
♥ *Louisa May Alcott*

For _____

From _____

Climbing into the
way-back machine
for a magical
mystery tour....

The Story of Your Life

Your date and place of birth: _____

_____

_____

_____

Who named you, and how was your name chosen? _____

_____

_____

_____

_____

_____

_____

_____

_____

_____

_____

Your parents' names, birthdates, and places of birth: _____

_____

_____

_____

_____

_____

_____

_____

_____

FAMILY FACES ARE MAGIC MIRRORS. LOOKING AT PEOPLE WHO BELONG TO US, WE SEE THE PAST, PRESENT & FUTURE. ♥ *Gail Lumet Buckley*

Your aunts and uncles: _____

_____

_____

_____

_____

Your brothers and sisters, oldest to youngest: _____

_____

_____

_____

_____

Who were you closest with in your family? _____

_____

_____

_____

_____

_____

_____

_____

_____

_____

_____

_____

_____

_____

A house is made of walls & beams; a home is built with love & dreams.

Do you know anything about the history of our family? From which country did we travel to America? Where did we settle? How did we get to where we are now?

Childhood...

What's your first memory? _____

_____

_____

_____

_____

_____

_____

_____

_____

YOUR
FIRST
HOUSE

What kind of child were you? _____

_____

_____

_____

_____

_____

_____

_____

_____

_____

_____

It's not that I belong to the past, but that the past belongs to me. ❤ Mary Antin

_____

_____

_____

_____

_____

_____

_____

_____

_____

_____

_____

_____

What is a special memory you have of your mother? _____

_____

_____

_____

_____

_____

_____

_____

_____

_____

_____

_____

_____

_____

_____

_____

_____

_____

_____

_____

_____

If you were to ask what is most important in a home, I would say memories. ♥ *Lillian Gish*

Tell me about your dad.

Tell me what you remember about your grandparents.

What were your favorite pastimes?

Did you play games with your family? If so, what were your favorites?

Did you have pets? _____

_____

_____

_____

_____

_____

_____

_____

_____

_____

_____

CUTE!

Describe your bedroom . . . did you share your room or have it all to yourself?

Did you have a television? What shows did you like to watch?

What was your favorite thing to eat? _____

_____

_____

_____

_____

_____

_____

_____

_____

_____

What was a special meal your mom made for you? _____

_____

_____

_____

_____

_____

_____

_____

_____

_____

_____

_____

Tell me about a memorable party or celebration. _____

Did you help around the house? Did you get an allowance? _____

Who were your childhood friends? _____

_____

_____

_____

_____

_____

_____

_____

_____

_____

Where did they live? _____

_____

_____

_____

_____

_____

_____

_____

_____

_____

_____

All those years ago...

What was your neighborhood like? _____

_____

_____

_____

_____

_____

_____

_____

_____

_____

_____

_____

_____

_____

_____

_____

_____

_____

_____

_____

_____

_____

ONE OF THE LUCKIEST THINGS
THAT CAN HAPPEN TO YOU IN LIFE
IS TO HAVE A HAPPY CHILDHOOD.
♥ Agatha Christie

Where did you first go to school? _____

_____

_____

_____

_____

_____

_____

_____

_____

_____

How did you get there? _____

_____

_____

_____

_____

_____

_____

_____

_____

_____

_____

_____

_____

Did you like school? Why? What were your most- and least-favorite subjects?
Who did you hang out with? _____

_____

_____

_____

_____

_____

_____

_____

_____

_____

_____

_____

_____

_____

_____

_____

_____

_____

_____

_____

_____

_____

_____

What were your favorite books?

What was your favorite kind of music? How did you listen to it? Did you go to concerts? Which ones?

_____

_____

_____

_____

_____

_____

_____

_____

_____

_____

_____

_____

_____

_____

_____

_____

_____

_____

_____

_____

HEIRLOOMS WE DON'T HAVE IN OUR FAMILY, BUT STORIES WE'VE GOT.
♥ Rose Chernin

What kinds of movies did you like? Which one could you watch every single day for the rest of your life? Who were your favorite movie stars? _____

_____

_____

_____

_____

_____

_____

_____

_____

_____

_____

_____

_____

_____

_____

_____

_____

_____

_____

_____

_____

Did you keep a diary? _____

_____

_____

_____

_____

_____

_____

_____

_____

_____

_____

Feel like divulging any family secrets? (I won't tell.) _____

_____

_____

_____

_____

_____

_____

_____

_____

_____

_____

_____

My Life

Are there any dreams from your childhood that you still remember?

What did you do during your summers? _____

_____

_____

_____

_____

_____

_____

_____

_____

_____

_____

_____

_____

_____

_____

_____

_____

_____

_____

_____

_____

Where did your family go on vacation? _____

_____

_____

_____

_____

_____

_____

_____

_____

_____

_____

_____

_____

_____

_____

_____

_____

_____

_____

_____

_____

_____

How did your family spend the holidays? _____

What were your favorite holiday foods? _____

_____

_____

_____

_____

_____

_____

_____

_____

_____

_____

_____

_____

_____

_____

_____

_____

_____

_____

_____

_____

_____

The best aromatherapy comes from the kitchen.

Will you share a favorite holiday recipe here?

Recipe: _____

Serves: _____

_____

_____

_____

_____

_____

_____

_____

_____

_____

_____

_____

_____

_____

_____

_____

_____

_____

_____

_____

_____

_____

_____

_____

Who was the clown of your family? What made you laugh? _____

_____

_____

_____

_____

_____

_____

_____

_____

_____

_____

_____

_____

_____

_____

_____

_____

_____

_____

_____

Did you like to dance? Did the dances have names? Give me some examples.
How did you learn the steps?

What did you do after school? Did you play sports or were you in any clubs?

_____

_____

_____

_____

_____

_____

_____

_____

_____

_____

_____

_____

_____

_____

_____

_____

_____

_____

Tell me about your religious upbringing. What were some memorable events?

What were the rules of the house? Curfews? _____

If you did something your parents didn't like, what were the consequences?

_____

_____

_____

_____

_____

_____

_____

_____

_____

_____

What did you do that flew under the radar, and you never got caught for it?

_____

_____

_____

_____

_____

_____

_____

_____

_____

_____

_____

_____

_____

Did you ever leave school with your friends without permission? _____

_____
_____
_____
_____
_____
_____
_____
_____
_____
_____
_____
_____
_____
_____
_____
_____
_____
_____
_____
_____
_____

IT'S SO EASY TO BE WICKED WITHOUT KNOWING IT, ISN'T IT?
♥ Anne Shirley / L.M. Montgomery

Who was your very best friend? How did you meet? What was your favorite song? Where'd you go, what'd you do, and who'd you see together?

Did you wear makeup? Or nail polish? What was a favorite outfit? _____

_____
_____
_____
_____
_____
_____
_____
_____
_____
_____
_____
_____
_____
_____
_____
_____
_____

in Tickle-Me Pink

We are not
interested
in the
possibilities
of defeat.
♥ Queen Victoria

How did you fix your hair? _____

_____

_____

_____

_____

_____

_____

_____

_____

_____

_____

TEENAGE YOU

What did you think you would be when you grew up? _____

_____
_____
_____
_____
_____
_____
_____
_____
_____
_____
_____
_____
_____
_____
_____
_____
_____
_____
_____
_____
_____
_____

What was the biggest thing you remember happening in our country when you were in high school? Who was president?

How old were you when you got your driver's license? What kind of car did you take the test in? How much was gas then? _____

_____

_____

_____

_____

_____

_____

_____

_____

_____

_____

_____

_____

_____

_____

_____

_____

_____

_____

_____

_____

_____

What's the best thing that's been invented since you were a kid? _____

_____

_____

_____

_____

_____

_____

_____

_____

_____

_____

_____

_____

_____

_____

_____

_____

_____

There are only two ways to live your
life. One is as though nothing
is a miracle. The other is
as if everything is.
♥ ALBERT EINSTEIN

Did you like fashion magazines? If not, what did you read for fun? _____

Did you ever think about what kind of house you wanted someday or where you might live? _____

_____

_____

_____

_____

_____

_____

_____

_____

_____

Or if you would get married, have children, or what kind of job you wanted?

_____

_____

_____

_____

_____

_____

_____

_____

_____

_____

Tell me about your first date: the who-what-where-when-and-why, all
the basics. How old were you? Where did you go, and what did you wear?
What did your parents have to say about all of this? _____

_____

_____

_____

_____

_____

_____

_____

_____

_____

_____

_____

_____

_____

_____

_____

_____

_____

_____

_____

_____

All grown up...

What did you do after high school? Did you go to college? _____

_____

_____

_____

_____

_____

_____

_____

_____

_____

_____

_____

_____

_____

_____

_____

_____

_____

_____

_____

_____

_____

What was your first place like? Did you live alone? _____

Did you like being on your own? _____

_____

_____

_____

_____

_____

_____

_____

_____

_____

_____

_____

_____

_____

_____

_____

_____

_____

_____

_____

_____

_____

Did you cook? What did you like to make? _____

_____

_____

_____

_____

_____

_____

_____

_____

_____

_____

_____

_____

_____

_____

_____

_____

_____

_____

_____

WHAT'S THE FRENCH FOR FIDDLE-DEE-DEE? ♥ LEWIS CARROLL

What was your first job? How much money did you make? What did you do?

What was your worst job ever? _____

_____

_____

_____

_____

_____

_____

_____

_____

_____

_____

_____

_____

_____

_____

_____

_____

_____

_____

_____

_____

_____

What did you do for fun? _____

_____

_____

_____

_____

_____

_____

_____

_____

_____

_____

_____

_____

_____

_____

_____

_____

_____

_____

_____

_____

_____

_____

Did you go on any road trips? _____

_____

_____

_____

_____

_____

_____

_____

_____

_____

Share some stories from that time... _____

_____

_____

_____

_____

_____

_____

_____

_____

_____

_____

_____

_____

Write a short page or two about the loves in your life, and anything you'd like to share...the good, the bad, the ugly, and the sublime.

Breathless, we flung us
    on the windy hill,
Laughed in the sun,
& kissed the lovely grass.
♥ Rupert Brooke

With all your expertise, can you give your best advice about relationships?

Was there one that got away? _____

_____

_____

_____

_____

_____

_____

_____

_____

_____

_____

_____

_____

_____

_____

_____

_____

_____

_____

_____

_____

♥ ♥ ♥ ♥ ♥ ♥ ♥ ♥ ♥ ♥ ♥ ♥ ♥ ♥ ♥ ♥

Did you ever fall in love at first sight? _____

_____

_____

_____

_____

_____

_____

_____

_____

_____

_____

_____

_____

_____

_____

_____

_____

_____

_____

_____

_____

_____

_____

_____

What was the most romantic date you ever went on? _____

_____

_____

_____

_____

_____

_____

_____

_____

_____

_____

_____

_____

_____

_____

_____

_____

_____

_____

_____

_____

I'll tell you how the sun rose,
A ribbon at a time. ♥ Emily Dickinson

Write about my grandfather and how you met him. How do you feel about him now?

Tell me about your first home together and having your first baby. Which year was that? _____

_____

_____

_____

_____

_____

_____

_____

_____

_____

_____

_____

_____

_____

_____

_____

_____

_____

_____

Ah! There is nothing like Staying home for real comfort.
♥ JANE AUSTEN

Did you enjoy being a mom? What was your favorite thing? _____

How was it when you brought home my dad/mom from the hospital? _____

Tell me about my parent as a child. _____

_____

_____

_____

_____

_____

_____

_____

_____

_____

_____

_____

_____

_____

_____

_____

_____

_____

_____

_____

_____

Did you also work outside of the house? (How did you find the time?!) _____

_____

_____

_____

_____

_____

_____

_____

_____

_____

_____

_____

_____

_____

_____

_____

_____

_____

_____

_____

_____

_____

IF YOU DON'T WANT YOUR CHILDREN TO HEAR WHAT YOU'RE SAYING, PRETEND YOU'RE TALKING TO THEM. ♥ ANON.

What kinds of hobbies, activities, and vacations did you enjoy as a grown-up?

YOU ON
VACATION

Where have you traveled that you love best, and why?

How did you spend your holidays? Which are your favorite of our
family traditions? _____

_____

_____

_____

_____

_____

_____

_____

_____

_____

_____

_____

_____

_____

_____

_____

_____

_____

_____

When you heard you were going to be a Grandma for the first time, how did you feel? How old were you when I was born? _____

_____

_____

_____

_____

_____

_____

_____

_____

_____

_____

_____

_____

_____

_____

_____

_____

_____

_____

_____

_____

_____

If I'd known how wonderful it would be to have grandchildren, I'd have had them first.
♥ Lois Wyse

Did you babysit for me?

What did we like to do, just the two of us? _____

_____

_____

_____

_____

_____

_____

_____

_____

_____

_____

_____

_____

_____

_____

_____

_____

_____

_____

_____

_____

Nobody can do for little children what grandmas do.
Grandmas sprinkle STARDUST over lives of little children.

What's the difference between your children and your grandchildren?

_____

_____

_____

_____

_____

_____

_____

_____

_____

_____

How are they similar? _____

_____

_____

_____

_____

_____

_____

_____

_____

_____

_____

_____

What's your secret food addiction? _____

_____

_____

_____

_____

_____

_____

_____

_____

_____

_____

_____

_____

_____

_____

_____

_____

_____

All the things I really like to do
are immoral, illegal, or fattening. ♥

What is a favorite family recipe of yours? Why is it special?

Will you write it down here?

Recipe: _____

Serves: _____

Did you grow flowers or vegetables in a garden? _____

_____

_____

_____

_____

_____

_____

_____

_____

_____

_____

_____

_____

_____

_____

_____

_____

_____

_____

_____

_____

_____

_____

TIME BEGAN
IN A GARDEN. ♥

What's your favorite quote, and why? _____

If you could be any age, which would you choose? _____

_____

_____

_____

_____

_____

_____

_____

_____

_____

_____

_____

_____

_____

_____

_____

_____

_____

_____

_____

_____

A loving heart is the truest wisdom.
♡ CHARLES DICKENS

What's a favorite piece of jewelry you own? Where did you get it? _____

If you could do it all over again, would you change anything? _____

_____

_____

_____

_____

_____

_____

_____

_____

_____

_____

_____

_____

_____

_____

_____

_____

_____

_____

No pessimist ever discovered the secrets of the stars, or sailed to an uncharted land, or opened a new heaven to the human spirit.
♥ Helen Keller

What hopes and dreams do you have for the future? _____

What would you most like to be remembered for? _____

_____

_____

_____

_____

_____

_____

_____

_____

_____

_____

_____

_____

_____

_____

_____

_____

_____

_____

_____

_____

All that mankind has done, thought or been:
it is in magic preservation, in the pages of books.
♥ THOMAS CARLYLE

What is your best advice about life?

There's absolutely no reason for being rushed along with the rush. Everybody should be free to go very slow.

Robt. Frost

What makes you the happiest? _____

_____

_____

_____

_____

_____

_____

_____

_____

_____

_____

_____

_____

_____

_____

_____

_____

_____

_____

_____

_____

_____

♥ ♥ ♥ ♥ ♥ ♥ ♥ ♥ ♥ ♥ ♥ ♥ ♥ ♥ ♥ ♥

What's the most important thing you have learned? _____

_____

_____

_____

_____

_____

_____

_____

_____

_____

_____

_____

_____

_____

_____

_____

_____

_____

_____

_____

_____

_____

_____

YOU
&
ME

Hours fly
Flowers die
New days
New ways
Pass by
Love stays

More stories...

(THAT'S MY STORY & I'M STICKING TO IT!)

_____

Sign your name

_____

Date